WORKING IN THE QUANTUM FIELD

BOOK ONE & BOOK TWO

APRIL AUTRY

COPYRIGHT © 2020

GALACTIC GRANDMOTHER®

https://GalacticGrandmother.com
https://info@galacticgrandmother.com

ISBN (ebook) 978-1-954785-007

ALSO BY APRIL AUTRY

Galactic Grandmother Past Life Series

ATLANTIS, JOURNEY FROM THE INNER TEMPLE

MY LIFE WITH JESUS

ESCAPE FROM MALDEK

Galactic Grandmother Spiritual Journey Series

MULTIDIMENSIONAL ASPECTS - HIGHER SELVES

BOOK ONE - CHAPTER 1

*A*t the age of nineteen I severely sprained my neck, commonly referred to as a whip lash injury, after flying over a sand dune in an off-road buggy. After that, I endured chronic neck problems, caused by instability in the muscles that support the cervical spine. Regular chiropractic adjustments, massage therapy and sleeping on a pillow that supports the neck, became my mainstays of treatment.

～

NOW IN MY SIXTIES, during a road trip out of state, I had forgotten to bring my cervical pillow. I awoke the first morning, after sleeping on a regular pillow, with a kink in my neck. I sat up in bed and began rubbing my neck, and my friend that shared the Airbnb room with me noticed. She asked what was wrong, and I told her it was just my neck reacting to a different pillow. Then she asked if she could do energy work on it.

"Of course!" I was happy for her help.

She sat on the side of my bed and asked me to relax while she quietly worked on me. Within five minutes, without touching my neck, she cleared the kink in my neck. All my discomfort had disappeared, and the miracle is, that my neck problems have never come back!

When she cleared the kink in my neck so quickly, I asked her what she did. I am a Reiki master and thought she may have used an energy technique similar to that. She told me that she was an Integrative Quantum Medicine practitioner, and that she had used quantum healing.

I knew immediately that I must learn how to do this! As it turned out, my friend also teaches IQM, so I signed up for her next class which just happened to be Level One.

As with all things my spirit guide has led me to, the synchronicity of manifesting the money for the class, airfare and rental car, along with having the time in my schedule to attend, worked out beautifully. The Integrative Quantum Medicine class opened my mind to the possibilities within the quantum field, and it was exciting. I returned home brimming with enthusiasm, knowing that quantum medicine was the next level of energy work.

Shortly thereafter, I was led to read a book by Kryon, The Twelve Layers of DNA, which teaches about the quantum connection to human DNA. Each day I looked forward to reading it as I sipped my morning coffee. I received many activations while learning about the quantum field and our multidimensionality.

As my experience with quantum healing progressed, I began receiving more and more downloads about quantum clearing, healing, and my multidimensional aspects that coexist in the quantum field. My inner guidance led me to develop my own form of quantum energy healing, which I have used successfully since. The information I present in this book is a small distillation of techniques to begin your understanding of, and working within, the quantum field. I recommend however, taking a class in quantum healing such as IQM to dive deeper.

My Venusian aspect told me, *"The quantum field is like soup, everything is there existing all at once, you make your intention for what or who you wish to connect with."*

. . .

INTENTION IS your navigation tool within the quantum field.

~

YOU MAY OBSERVE similarities between meditation and other techniques that work while in a relaxed state. When we relax and allow our mind to drift away from third dimensional awareness, such as our daily activities and worries, we slip into higher dimensions that exist within the quantum field. Accessing higher dimensions is natural to us. We do this when we day dream, use our imagination, sleep, get into the zone with sports, and meditate. You have learned to access higher dimensions, yet you may not have realized you were actually within the multidimensionality of the quantum field.

Your first impression of quantum healing may be that it is too easy to be real. I assure you that it is very real, and the fact that it seems too easy to be real, is only because you are not yet aware of how powerful you are. We are fractals of Creator Source energy, and as such we are Creator Beings. We literally manifest our reality. As you learn to work with mindful intention in the quantum field, you will realize your power.

The caveat to personal power, is that your power is increased as the frequency of your consciousness is elevated. The true law of attraction is about energetic resonance, and the omniscience of the Divine Creator/God recognized that power belongs to those that would not abuse it. This means that you must do the inner work to clear and heal yourself. As you clear density or lower vibrational energies, you are able to hold and integrate more light or higher vibrational energies.

Whatever energy you hold within, such as your thoughts and emotions, is the type of energy that you will attract. Selfish motivations will manifest selfishness being directed toward you. If you have a loving heart, this will attract loving, joyful experiences that are in resonance with the energy you emit. As we embody our higher spiritual energies, we acquire an unselfish perspective, along with personal power that manifests what is best for all.

~

WE MUST CONSCIOUSLY INITIATE and work toward our spiritual development. We must signal to our Higher Self or spirit guides that we are ready to learn and begin the path of self-discovery. In this book, I will give you techniques to do personal quantum clearing and healing, to assist you on a path of self-discovery.

As you use these techniques, you may begin receiving activations and downloads of your own. Your intuition and spiritual understanding will improve, and you may find that your relationships, life and health are also improving. All this comes with using your abilities as a conscious co-creator of your life in the multidimensional quantum field.

BOOK ONE - CHAPTER 2

As a fractal of Divine Source energy, we have ALL that is perfect within us. We are pure love energy at our core Self, and within the quantum field, we may access more of who we are.

With each incarnation, each individualized experience, we build a container of likes, dislikes, phobias, talents, etc. that become that which we call our soul. Our soul is the unique consciousness that we carry from lifetime to lifetime. We carry the residual of experiences that have been both painful and joyful. Unfortunately the negative emotions that remain with us, along with painful childhood experiences from this lifetime, can unconsciously motivate us in our daily life. These unconscious motivations are often referred to as inner child issues.

It is true that our inner child holds our hurt, anger, jealousy, insecurity, and other negative emotional energies for us, yet our inner child is also loving, playful, creative, inquisitive, and delights in the small things of life. When we begin destructive behaviors such as self-sabotaging relationships, acquiring addictions to alcohol, drugs, sex or eating, we must address what our inner child is holding and clear it. This inner child work is also referred to as inner work or shadow work. Once the destructive energies in our life are cleared, we can appreciate the positive attributes of our inner child, and integrate it with love for all it has done on our behalf.

"How do I do this?" You might ask. "How do I clear out lifetimes of negative energy that are currently causing me problems?"

~

THERE ARE many techniques to start your inner work. The first is recognizing your attitudes and emotions. Which negative attitudes or emotions do you display? Do you feel like a victim to circumstances or people? Do you get angry easily? Observe how you react to people and things. Look at the emotions that surface, such as fear, insecurity, jealousy, resentment, or anger. Start simply by addressing what is in your life now. Consider whether these are your own genuine emotions, or whether you have taken on emotional energy from others. We often identify with other people's miseries, or the injustices they endure, then hold these energies within us.

Start a journal and write down what is bothering you. You may find certain emotions or topics reoccur, or you may identify patterns of behavior that need clearing. Organizing your thoughts in this way fights feeling overwhelmed. When you make a list, you can address each item, and see your progress as you work to clear or heal them. While some issues may be on-going, you will acknowledge that you are doing what you can now, and this builds self-confidence.

Reading self-help books, journaling, past-life regression therapy, counseling, classes, meditation, physical exercise, acupuncture, energy therapies, and massage therapy are all signals to your inner self, that you have set the intention to grow mentally, emotionally, spiritually and physically into your highest potential. You wish to clear out all that no longer serves your personal evolution.

~

TELL yourself what your intentions are. Tell yourself that you will not waste your time and energy, on suffering and being unhappy. It is your choice, and you can decide which path you will take. Begin communication with your Higher Self, angels, spirit guides, Divine Creator, God, or whomever you identify as working with you for your highest good. You may not hear an answer at first, but rest assured you are being heard, and you will receive guidance.

Start by understanding that you are the Creator of your own universe. Each decision that you make now, affects not only your present reality, but also your future timeline. Seemingly small choices, whether about food, exercise, work or relationships can change your timeline for tomorrow.

What does your perfect day look like? How would it differ from your usual day, and what changes can you make today? Do you have negative thoughts about yourself or others? Do you put off taking that walk or eating healthy foods? You can start small and slowly incorporate what you'd like. Don't judge yourself harshly, encourage yourself as you would a child starting something new.

∾

AFTER YOU LEARN to access the quantum field, you can do personal clearing and healing. This isn't to say that clearing an issue is always instantaneous, because there may be deeper layers that need to be cleared, or time needed to release the energies.

Serious injuries, disease, pain, emotional, mental, and spiritual issues may be cleared, unless they are needed to continue an incarnational lesson for spiritual growth. We will begin with a basic energy clearing, where you will learn to use your intentions and visualization to work in the quantum field.

ENERGY FIELD CLEARING

1. Sit or lie in a comfortable position. Take in and blow out four slow deep breaths, and as you do, feel your body relax.
2. Visualize your entire body relaxed, from your feet all the way up to the top of your head.
3. **State clearly: All energies that DO NOT belong to me, leave me now and return to Source/God for transmutation.** You may state either Source or God, depending on what feels better to you.
4. Sit or lie for a few moments, allowing all foreign energies to leave.
5. **State clearly: All energies that DO belong to me, that no longer serve my highest and best good, leave me now and return to Source/God for transmutation.**
6. Sit or lie for a few moments, allowing all the energies that you no longer need to leave.
7. **Visualize white light within you and extending out several feet, See the light surrounding your entire body.**
8. **State clearly: I AM a sovereign Being of Light and Love. I AM protected by ALL that I AM.**
9. **And so, it begins.**

~

I no longer say and "so it is". That saying has a connotation of finality. I now say and "so it begins".

This energy clearing can be used as many times a day as you need. If you are an empath, you may find it useful after being in group situations, as you easily pick up other people's energies.

Suggested minimal usage is daily prior to sleep.

BOOK ONE - CHAPTER 3

$\mathscr{F}$reedom is our birth right. Freedom to think, freedom to feel, and freedom to create. We are fractals of the greatest Creator of All, Divine Source, God, and as such we should never have limitations put upon the expansion of our consciousness.

The first step in expanding one's consciousness is to break out of our mind programming. Education, family, culture, religion have all played a part in your belief system of what is possible. We have been trained to believe that what we see, hear, smell, taste and touch are the only senses that humans are capable of. We have been indoctrinated to think and believe in ways that belong to herd mentality. If we question the status quo, we are labeled with derogatory terms. We are seen as a threat to the herd reality, rather than innovators.

Our minds have the capability to expand our conscious awareness into the quantum field. When we begin to direct our intentions into the quantum field, we are able to direct energy and heal our physical body and maintain a high vibration that resists disease. We are able to clear emotional wounds and ways of thinking that hold us back from achieving our highest potential.

All this and more, is possible if we break out of the boxes that confine our thinking. I will lead you in the mind box removal, that may seem too simple to work, yet it is an important step in learning to use your conscious intention within the quantum field.

MIND BOX REMOVAL

1. Focus your attention to your breath. Breathe deeply into your nose, expanding your lungs, then blow out through your mouth. With each breath, feel your body relax.
2. Envision a small sun or ball of light in the middle of your chest. Take in a big breath and see the light in your chest expand, then blow out the air. With each breath in, the light in your chest becomes bigger, until it expands out to the sides of your chest.
3. Envision a box that sits on top of your head. The box is firmly attached to the top of your head.
4. Take in a deep breath and when you exhale, envision that you blow the light from your chest up through your head and into the box.
5. See the box fill with light, then explode.
6. Do that again. Take in a big breath and blow the light from your chest through your head into the box.
7. See the box fill with light, then explode into small particles out into infinity.
8. Now see your head free and clear from the box.

9. **State clearly: I am open to receive from my Higher Self, angels, and spirit guides.**
10. **State clearly: I will not immediately reject new ideas. I will use discernment and allow my Higher Self to guide me to greater understanding.**
11. **State clearly: I now begin the process of enlightenment and remembrance of who I AM.**
12. **And so, it begins.**

∾

If you feel tingling above your head, you're just feeling your own energy body, that has been stimulated by your focused attention. If you don't feel anything, that is fine. Each person reacts differently to energy work.

By removing your mind box, you have done a clearing of old programming that hindered the expansion of your consciousness. You may find the need to repeat this clearing, as acquired ways and patterns of thinking will continue to show themselves. If you find yourself doing negative self-talk or self-criticism, do the mind box clearing immediately and set an intention that all negative self-talk or criticism ends now.

Many believe they are small, ineffectual, unimportant, not good enough, and the list of negative attributes goes on. However, all this is programming. Programming that hinders your evolution in every way, spiritual, mental, physical and emotional. Now is the time to eliminate barriers in your life, as these hinderances do not reflect who you REALLY are. You are a Divine co-creator of your life, as such you will leave behind all that no longer serves you and incorporate all those things that will assist you to achieve your highest potential.

BOOK ONE - CHAPTER 4

*O*ur gut feelings, voice of conscience, feeling that something or someone just isn't right, are senses that are as natural to humans as the sense of taste. These elusive feelings are actually our intuition. What is intuition? Intuition is connected to our soul through countless incarnations that have taught us to read the energies of people and situations.

Through many lifetimes, we have strengthened our sense of intuition. Some people have a stronger intuition than others, even psychic in their ability to read others or make predictions based on what they energetically pick up. However, since intuition is part of our multidimensional nature, we can become more mindful of our intuition and develop it as we work in the quantum field.

First, you must set the intention to be mindful, and acknowledge when you receive messages or feelings from your intuition. Often your first reaction to your intuition, will be your mind telling you why your gut feeling is wrong. An example is, you meet a new person and your immediate feeling is, "I don't like him/her." or "I can't trust this person." Then your mind tells you, "You don't know this person." or, "Don't be judgmental." Later, you learn that you don't like this person because he/she turned out to be dishonest and wasn't trustworthy.

Our heart and our mind often cause conflict over decisions. An example of this, is your mind telling you that the person you are in a relationship with is perfect for you. Your mind says this person has all the qualities that you were looking for in a partner, and that you would be crazy not to continue the relationship. However, your heart tells you that something is missing. This person doesn't meet your emotional needs, and no matter how hard you've tried to love this person, you just don't feel committed to them and want to break-up. Your friends and family tell you that love will come or give the relationship another chance. What do you do?

$$\sim$$

IF I TOLD you that your soul speaks to you through your intuition, your feelings or your heart, would that make the decision to break-up easier? In truth, your soul is directly connected to you through your heart, and you have a heart portal, which is the energetic link between you and your multidimensional higher selves.

If you are experiencing strong feelings about someone or something, your soul is speaking to you. In my own experience when I was 30, I had the perfect child with the perfect husband and father, lived in a perfect house, with all that I believed I needed to be happy. Yet, I was being forced out of this situation by my feelings. I had no good reason to leave my so-called perfect life, yet it seemed my happiness depended on it. I experienced a huge battle between my head and heart, or my mind and feelings, before finally making the decision to leave my marriage and move away with my child.

At that time, I did not know my pre-incarnation plan was to meet my second husband and have another child by him. My feelings made me so miserable, that I had to leave everything, in order to continue my life's plan. My soul was making sure that I continued in the right direction for my spiritual growth. In retrospect, I also went through a huge initiation which catapulted me out of certain cultural and familial programming.

～

YOU WILL REACH the point when your heart and mind are in sync. This will occur after you have embodied enough higher spiritual energy to raise your frequency. Once you have done this, you will be working in co-operation with your higher aspects, and your perspective will have changed so that your heart and mind see things without selfish motivations and polarity.

Don't be discouraged, if you are reading this book, your journey to enlightenment has already begun. Next, I will lead you in an exercise to anchor intentions for your spiritual growth.

STATEMENT OF INTENTIONS

If you are outside, look around at nature with gratitude in your heart. If you are inside, light a candle or incense and set the mood for a sacred ceremony.

Settle into a comfortable position and close your eyes.

1. Take four slow deep breaths in and out through your nose.
2. Feel your entire body relax from your toes to the top of your head.
3. Take in a slow deep breath and direct it to your heart center. Then blow out.
4. Repeat this breath into and out of your heart center four times.
5. With eyes closed, focus your attention to your heart.

State clearly:

**I AM ready to receive activations and upgrades,
I AM ready to embody more LOVE and LIGHT.**

Repeat again:

I AM ready to receive activations and upgrades,
I AM ready to embody more LOVE and LIGHT.
And so, it begins.

BOOK ONE - CHAPTER 5

*a*ll the above exercises have been statements to your higher dimensional aspects within the quantum field. You are beginning conscious communication with your Higher Self, angels, guides or spiritual team of personal helpers. From this point forward, you should continue the conversation with spirit. Ask for guidance, ask for signs they are with you, ask to remember your dreams, or meditate with the intention to receive a message.

There is a universal law that we are allowed free choice, and those in higher dimensions may not interfere with our choices. They must wait for us to ask for their help. You have stated that you are open to receive their assistance for your spiritual discovery and growth.

Our misconception is that we are disconnected from spirit, that we are alone to navigate our life, yet waiting on the sidelines are those available to help. Our spiritual team is always ready and willing to do what they can on our behalf. They see the larger picture, they know what our life plan is, and they will guide you to learn what you need to know.

When I look back at the guidance that I have received, I see each step I've taken as a piece of a patchwork quilt. My Higher Self has guided me to expand my consciousness from one subject to the next, before finally pulling it all together in a beautiful quilt of knowledge.

The Pleiadian Council of Nine represent the Pleiadian collective and are tasked with disseminating spiritual concepts to the collective consciousness here on Earth. During meditation, I was led by this Council to light a candle, and perform a sacred ceremony of releasing all karmic energies. When I was finished, I was told that I am completely free of karma and in each new moment I will decide my future timeline and karmic energies.

My disclaimer is that an individual's pre-incarnation plan, may or may not allow a complete release of all karma.

COMPREHENSIVE KARMA RELEASE

1. Settle into a comfortable position. Take four slow deep breaths in and out through your nose.
2. Feel your body relax and your mind free from thoughts.
3. **State Clearly: In ALL time, space, dimensions, parallel realities and universes;**

I release all karmic energies that belong to me.

I release all karmic energies that don't belong to me.

I release all karmic energies with animals and plants.

I release all karmic energies with fresh and sea water animals and fish.

I release all karmic energies with the collective consciousness.

I release all karmic energies with family, children and ancestors.

I release all karmic energies with physical disease and traumatic injuries.

I release all karmic energies that are the light of my own soul, and that has kept me trapped or bound to old spiritual paradigms.

I release all karmic energies to off world entities and extraterrestrials.

I release all karmic energies to people that may want to manip-
ulate or use me.

I release any karma on all universes, galaxies, parallel realities,
time, space, dimensions past, present and future.

I release all karmic energies to Mother Gaia/Earth.

I release all karmic energies to the moon and other planets
where I have lived or had experiences.

I release all karmic energies to collective consciousness trauma
from natural and manmade causes.

BOOK ONE - CHAPTER 6

*T*he **Energy Field Clearing, Mind Box Removal, Statement of Intentions,** and **Comprehensive Karma Release**, plus the information given, are invaluable steps on your path to self-discovery. My recommendation is that you read each chapter again and again, each time practicing the techniques, until you can easily do them on your own. These techniques prepare you for deeper quantum work, and as you process the information, your own downloads will begin.

At this point, you need to be practicing meditation for ten to thirty minutes each day, as a way to "check-in" with your Higher Self, guides, angels or spiritual team.

Again, I recommend a journal to accompany your inner work of clearing old denser energies, and also to record the downloads of information that you may begin receiving in meditations.

Spend thirty to sixty minutes a day reading, you will be guided to at least a couple of books that will benefit your spiritual, emotional, and/or mental growth. Watch videos on social media, there are videos on any subject that you may be interested in, and many qualified teachers that offer information free of charge.

Be a mindful observer of yourself. Watch how you react to everything, from family to strangers, and to circumstances. You are not a victim and no one else is responsible for your actions or reactions.

All the time, energy, money, and effort that you put forth to expand your consciousness, learn more about who you are and why you are here, is the best investment that you can make. These investments pay off not only in this lifetime, but in future lifetimes. You also affect your past and future ancestral lineage, and your growth always uplifts the collective consciousness. We are in this together. Whether you realize it yet or not, we are all spiritual family.

BOOK TWO - CHAPTER 1

*W*orking in the Quantum Field, Book Two is about the physicality of enlightenment. You can work with the innate physical consciousness through intention and through speaking to your body. You are the Creator in physical form, you are the directing Spirit within the body, and your body's consciousness is awaiting your acknowledgement and directions. This is a quantum/multidimensional truth, not just an esoteric concept. Living as a conscious human being requires mental, emotional and spiritual awareness, and also includes honoring and respecting your body.

This book guides you through physical quantum techniques. We have been experiencing lifetimes with pre-installed physical templates, that support disease and death as a way to end life, after which a new incarnation could begin for further lessons and wisdom building. However, we are at a point in our consciousness evolution, when we can program our own physical templates. We can access our akash, or acquired talents and knowledge, within the quantum field and bring what we need into this lifetime. When we understand our multidimensional nature, we can work in the quantum field to improve our current life and accelerate our spiritual enlightenment.

In East Indian yogic traditions, an enlightened yogi will

consciously and intentionally leave their body, in what is called maha-samadhi. This is death of the physical body and exit of the light body back into the spiritual dimensions by choice. Lahiri Mahasaya's maha-samadhi was documented by his followers, and he was said to have turned around three times, before facing the north in a lotus position and entering his final maha-samadhi.

Whether the yogi intuitively knows the physical body is ready to expire, or the yogi chooses the time of death, it would seem that years of meditation practices, and inner work, had prepared the yogi to travel in the light body or merkaba from the physical plane into the spiritual planes.

Maha-samadhi is an example of the mind-body energetic connection in the extreme. When I say mind, I am referring to consciousness. When I say mind-body, I am referring to the way your consciousness affects your physical body. In the case of the enlightened yogi, his consciousness was in alignment with higher spiritual energy. He used the power of his consciousness to direct his light body to leave the physical body.

~

PHYSICAL BEHAVIORS such as stress eating, unconsciously tapping a foot or biting your fingernails are also examples of the mind-body connection. The mind-body connection is important to learn about, because you are continuously programing and commanding your body, whether consciously or unconsciously.

Your commands can be positive, such as "I am strong and able to accomplish what I desire."

Or your commands may be negative, such as "I am weak and sickly."

The programs and commands that you send your body should be positive at all times. Your mind/consciousness should support your body, not tear it down. Mental and emotional distress such as worrying, post-traumatic stress, grieving, regret, anger, jealousy, or resentment among others, can cause physical illness or disease if the distress is not cleared.

There are many techniques to resolve distress which include counseling or therapy and quantum healing done by yourself or others. Sometimes allowing another to help, gives you a different perspective to initiate healing. However, learning to work in the quantum field, will allow you to clear, heal and reprogram your body through conscious commands. Other techniques to access the quantum field are meditation, hypnosis, shamanic journeys, and past life regressions.

~

THE PHYSICAL BODY literally EMBODIES spirit. This means that the quality of consciousness that you hold IN YOUR BODY will affect the physical changes you can make. Envision each cell in your body holding energy or energetic frequencies. This energy could be dark, dense low vibrational energy or higher vibrational light energy. As we clear out lower, dark energies such as bad attitudes, selfish behaviors, mental or emotional distress, those energies leave our physical cells and are replaced with light energy.

As your physical cells hold more and more light, your body's frequency rises. When your physical cells vibrate at a fifth dimensional or higher frequency, you no longer are susceptible to lower frequency illness. This is a huge statement about health, and there will always be caveats to contradict it, yet if your pre-incarnation life plan does not include a karmic disease or trauma, excellent health and long life may be a benefit of doing inner work.

As you progress, your physical body is more light-filled with a higher energetic frequency, which makes you more sensitive to incoming solar and planetary energies. You may become sensitive to energies from Mother Earth, such as crystals, plants and water. Your hand chakras may activate, you may begin to channel higher frequency energies, and become interested in energy healing such as Reiki.

Physical movement becomes extremely important at this stage in your development. The body needs to move the energies through or discharge the energies, and also eliminate stagnant energy. Simple exercise such as walking or more strenuous exercise, could be used to clear your body. Some form of physical movement should be as much a part of your daily routine as meditation.

~

YOUR SPIRITUAL DEVELOPMENT requires inner and outer work. You must bring together the mental, emotional, spiritual and physical energies to work in unison toward your enlightenment.

We are multi-faceted, multidimensional, and our growth depends on balancing all of what we are. We can't only study spirituality, we can't only be academic, or physically oriented. Have faith that your intuition, Higher Self, or Divine guidance will assist you to integrate everything as needed.

You will receive DNA upgrades, activations, and initiations at the perfect time. You will be guided to what you need to know, through ideas that intrigue or excite you. You may experience difficult people or circumstances that initiate self-reflection and growth, as well as, experiences that are joy filled, loving and expand your heart center.

BOOK TWO - CHAPTER 2

*I*n **Working in the Quantum Field Book One**, you were given techniques to clear your energy field, mind box, state your intentions for spiritual growth, and release old karmic programming. Now we will address the old physical template that was pre-installed into our bodies prior to incarnation.

Throughout our evolution, the purpose of reincarnation was to experience and learn, and we needed a physical program that would terminate our body. Our original physical template allowed our bodies to easily live for hundreds of years, which we did in ancient times, and was referenced in the Bible. At some point, a physical template was programed into our body consciousness to shorten the body's life. With the body dying earlier, humanity could reincarnate quicker, and accelerate the wisdom gained in each lifetime.

There may be questions about a dark agenda and this new template, however, suffice it to say humanity has benefited from the shortened lifetimes. Over thousands of years, the collective consciousness has been given the opportunity to have an increased amount of experiences, that led to greater understanding, compassion, empathy and a more loving consciousness. This was a slow evolution, the dense consciousness was pierced with light, when horrific events such as burning witches were able to open the hearts of people that watched, or plagues and wars caused people to work together.

With evolutionary advancements, humanity has developed many kinds of spiritual concepts, higher ideals and integrity, and learned about care and treatment of the body. The body is living longer due to this, and due to treating the body as a "temple" for the soul or spirit.

Many have studied the energetic needs of the light body and the physical body, so at this time, we are able to present a new template. This template is not to be taken without serious consideration, as you will be accepting full responsibility for the welfare of your body. You will remove the old programming, and be the one directing your physical consciousness, so you will need to learn how to communicate with your body. In Chapter Three, I will teach you the O-Ring technique to communicate with your body, which can be used as you continue to develop your intuitive powers.

∼

PLEASE DEDICATE TIME TO make a sacred ceremony for releasing your old physical programming. Ensure that you will not be disturbed, light a candle or some incense, and state an intention that you are making a serious commitment to work with your body consciousness for the highest good. Of course, this can be done outside in nature, with gratitude and love for all Mother Gaia has provided.

Start by assuming a comfortable position, breath deeply and slowly in and out, until your mind and body are relaxed and in a meditative state. Then mindfully read each line. Do not rush, take the time to absorb the meaning of the words. After you finish reading through it, begin again and repeat reading until you feel you have integrated it.

RELEASING OLD PHYSICAL PROGRAMING

I AM on the perfect path for my spiritual evolution.

I AM guided by my connection to the Divine and by my Higher Self.

I AM consciously expanding my awareness and moving forward to my highest potential.

I thank my body's guidance for assisting me to this present point in my evolution.

I thank my DNA for guiding the program for my spiritual evolution.

I thank my physical consciousness and DNA for driving my spiritual evolution forward, through the death and reincarnation process until now, and I am in gratitude to you.

I AM ready to release the old physical program.

I now release any old energy, karmic energy, DNA programing, and innate consciousness associated with the death and reincarnation process.

I now release any old energy, karmic energy, DNA programing, and innate consciousness associated with disease of the physical body.

I no longer need disease to spiritually evolve.

I no longer need death to spiritually evolve.

I release all old programing and the old template about spiritual evolution through disease, physical death and dying.

From this point forward I will continue to grow and spiritually evolve, according to the guidance of my Higher Self.

I will live in this body in a state of physical excellence, both in health and vibrant energy.

I will decide when I will pass from this body based on my highest consciousness.

I love my old physical innate consciousness and programing, and hereby release it back to Source.

I love my old karmic energy and DNA programing, and hereby release it back to Source.

Take a deep breath, blow out, and say out loud:

As of now, I AM the Master Creator of my own spiritual evolution, and so it begins.

BOOK TWO - CHAPTER 3

a simple way of communicating with your body is the O-ring technique, which can be used while you develop your intuitive powers of communicating with your body. You will ask your body to reply to statements such as, "Salad would be good for lunch," or "Fish would be beneficial for dinner." Your body will give simple yes or no answers. Do not believe for an instant, that your body doesn't have preferences. Even if you know salad may be good for lunch, your body may prefer or need a different kind of food.

You should respect your body's wishes and work in cooperation with it. There will be times when you will really want something, yet your body doesn't. I go along with my body 95% of the time, yet if I want that piece of birthday cake or celebratory glass of champagne, I will respectfully tell my body that I am going to enjoy eating or drinking that item. After all, we are supposed to enjoy our life, and sometimes that includes birthday cake! The point is, that we are mindful of the fuel we provide our body.

There will be times when the physical body needs more protein and will crave animal or fish proteins in addition to plant proteins. There will be times when the physical body is repulsed by animal or fish proteins, turning toward fruit and vegetables to satisfy and fulfill its needs. It is important to remain nonjudgmental with regards to your body's choices, and with regards to other people's choices. There is no one answer about what is best, or the spiritually superior choice. What is right for one person, may not be for another. When I asked my higher guidance for an answer about whether eating meat was wrong, this is the answer that I received.

CHANNELING ON WHETHER TO EAT MEAT

Earth, oceans, plants, animals, humans, and every other thing is composed of the same Creator Source energy. One energy is not superior to another. When we, and I include all life such as plants, animals, fishes, trees, choose to be a fractal of the ALL/Source/Creator energy on this Being planet, Gaia, we enter into the contract of becoming part of nature's cycle of life here.

Plants grow and are harvested and eaten. They willingly give their life energy to sustain life in whatever eats it. Fishes and animals do the same. They live their life and accept the end of their life as part of nature, whether they are killed and eaten by another animal or killed and eaten by a human. The energy with which an animal, fish or plant is killed or harvested makes the difference as to whether it is high vibrational or not.

If a Native American kills a deer to eat its flesh, and use its bones and skin, the animal's life is honored and thanked. The energy is high because gratitude is given for the animal's life. Eskimos have sustained themselves by eating whales. This does not make them less spiritual than others. Indigenous peoples have hunted, fished, and gathered plants to live according to natural law.

The problem with eating animals and fishes started when the

animals and fishes were not treated with gratitude, when they were tortured and put in states of fear before their death. That energy is very low, and transfers into our own bodies. As a collective in the future, we humans will decide that we no longer need to eat the flesh of animals or fishes.

In the future, we will sustain our human energy by plant products that are grown in abundance with love, and in amounts that will feed all humans on the planet. Until that timeline manifests, we must consider that any philosophical judgement about what another should or should not eat is not ours to make. Any judgement that is made must apply to all humans on the planet. In other words, we cannot judge another that needs to kill an animal or fish to eat, when that is what is needed or available to feed themselves. If we are not providing all humans on the planet with foods, then we cannot judge another's choices.

Philosophically, there are large numbers of humans in touch with the future timeline that does not consume animals or fishes, and for those people it is right and correct to follow their own conscious food choices. Yet, one must remember that our physical bodies have consciousness as well. Yes, we are the creators of our own realities and thus can make the choice not to eat flesh, yet if one is in alignment with one's own physical energetic needs, currently there will be times when the body may need protein in the form of flesh.

End of Transmission

BOOK TWO - CHAPTER 4

Quantum eating is mindful eating, as you are mindful of the energies that the food brings into your body. Eating fresh produce, grown in the fields absorbing sunshine, water, and nutrients from the earth bring clean energies into your body. Eating genetically modified foods that were grown in soil filled with weed killer, sprayed above ground with pesticides, then manufactured into food products with preservatives, chemicals to retain or make flavor, and non-food products that make textures or colors, are bringing nothing into your body except toxins or pollutants for your body to process and clear out. However, your body cannot clear out all the toxins and will store them in your body, which afterwards may cause disease.

Our culture has been manipulated into thinking that fast food is a quick and healthy way to feed our families, when in fact, it has shortened the life expectancy of our children. The hamburgers, chicken, fish, fries, sodas, deserts, and other prepared food have been adulterated with chemicals, oils and non-food products you would never eat if not disguised as food. In fact, fast food contains addictive additives to keep you coming back for more.

We must also consider products that we apply to our skin. The skin is the largest organ of our body, and harmful chemicals contained in lotions, deodorants, shampoos, cosmetics and hair color can also cause disease. Some cancerous breast tumors have been found to contain toxic ingredients from certain deodorants. Ideally, you should be mindful of all energies that come into your field, whether through food, drink, media, sound, or whomever you allow into your energetic field through sex.

~

THE O-RING MUSCLE test has been extensively used as an Applied Kinesiology tool to test muscles. Traditional Chinese Medicine kinesiology evaluates the relationship between the meridians to address body imbalances. Both styles of kinesiology work with the body's natural electrical grid.

In quantum medicine the O-ring technique is taken a step further. Your fingers relay communication from your Higher Self, and allows self-testing for your body.

When you first learn the O-ring technique, it is important to make the connection between your inner guidance and your fingers. To do this, you will enter into a meditative state with the intention of getting answers with your fingers. After you have made a firm connection with your fingers and inner guidance, you won't need the meditative state. Just telling yourself that you are in alignment with your inner guidance and will receive answers with your fingers will be enough.

I recommend that you practice the O-ring technique until your yes and no answers are decisive. Your body knows what it needs from a nutritional and an energetic perspective, so at that point, I recommend that you make a list of all foods, beverages, and body products such as lotions, etc. that you apply to your skin, then go through and test each one to see if your body believes those items are beneficial or not. Your body's needs change, and one day, week, or month your body may want a certain food, then the next it won't. This will become your baseline. After I did this, I posted the food and beverage list on my refrigerator, and it reminded me to work with my body consciousness daily.

O-RING TECHNIQUE

1. Take slow deep breaths in and out to relax your body and clear your mind.
2. If you are right-handed, use your left thumb and index finger to make a circle.
3. Use your right thumb or index finger to tug inside the circle. If you are left-handed switch the positions and see if that feels better.
4. **State: "I am in alignment with my inner guidance, my fingers will give me answers."**

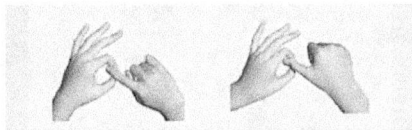

You do not need to hold your circle tightly, nor tug hard with the other hand. Experiment with pressure. Say, "Show me yes." Then tug at your circle. If your circle stays closed, that is yes. Then say, "Show me no." Then tug at your circle. If your circle opens and allows your finger or thumb to come through, that is no. You may find that your personal yes and no are opposite from this, what is important is that yes and no are consistent. Practice asking your fingers to show you yes and no until you have trained your fingers.

Next say "My name is _____" using your name, then tug at your circle. Your fingers should answer yes. Double check by saying "My name is ____" and use a name that isn't yours. Your fingers should say no.

You have just learned the most useful tool of working in the quantum field with your body consciousness, at least until you have fine-tuned your intuition. When asking your fingers for answers, always listen for your inner voice of intuition. You may find your inner voice answers prior to your fingers, and that your fingers confirm the answer you heard. Strengthen your intuition by listening for it.

BOOK TWO - CHAPTER 5

*Y*ou have released the old template for your physical body, and you have learned to communicate with your body consciousness, so what is next? I recommend that you begin a complete detox and rejuvenation of your body, along with the inner work that you began in Book One.

You may start a separate journal for your physical body, in which you record the baseline of what your body wants to eat, drink and allow on its skin. You can include exercises, or physical movement such as hiking or swimming, your weight and general physical condition. I believe that you will see much improvement as time and your relationship with your body consciousness develops. You may happily record the last days of allergies, headaches, aches and illness as your health improves through conscious intention.

When detoxing, I believe in a gentle approach. My personal opinion is that we don't need to shock our body, instead we can lovingly guide it. Start by cutting out the processed foods and sodas, and find healthy, whole food replacements. Your body knows what to do with whole foods such as fruits and vegetables, juices, teas and water infused with herbs and fruits.

You should consider decreasing sugar and caffeine. I drink a cup of black coffee every morning, yet this was an acquired taste. Like others, I once drank the oil-based sugar laden creamers, that taste so good yet are terrible for your health. Many people are literally addicted to the expensive drinks offered by a famous coffee chain and find themselves needing to go out each day for their fix.

Alcohol is a part of our lives, used for many reasons, and very often because we enjoy the flavor. However, it has been abused and should be seriously considered with regards to your intentions. Drinking alcohol in a mindful way, without excess, such as during a special meal, ceremony, or toasting a joyful occasion carries positive energy. Making the alcohol yourself, perhaps from grapes you have grown and imbued with love and appreciation, carries an even higher energy. Yet, you should always use discernment with your personal choice regarding alcohol, and communicate with your body conscious-ness about its preferences.

REJUVENATION of your body will happen naturally as you consciously work with your body, giving it what it needs, and avoiding what it doesn't. Nurturing yourself in body, mind and spirit is why I wrote these books. During my own spiritual journey, I have found that inner work begets happiness through better relationships and understanding of Self, while the physical work begets excellent health through supporting the body's needs. My greatest wish for you is that your life improves as mine has. Much love and blessings for excellent results.

ABOUT THE AUTHOR

April Autry

April writes about her spiritual journey, including many of her past lives.

April is an intuitive mentor, Quantum healer, Reiki master, yoga teacher, marriage minister, and teaches alignment of your mind-body-soul through consciousness expansion and spiritual practices.

Books, meditations, courses and spiritual lifestyle products can be found on her website:

https://GalacticGrandmother.com

April enjoys reading your book reviews, so please feel free to email her at:

https://info@galacticgrandmother.com

www.ingramcontent.com/pod-product-compliance
Lightning Source LLC
LaVergne TN
LVHW052039080426
835513LV00018B/2393